Wild Women of a Certain Age

Wild Women of a Certain Age

Magi Gibson

Chapman Publishing

2000

Chapman Publishing
4 Broughton Place
Edinburgh EH1 3RX
Scotland

The publisher acknowledges the award
from the Deric Bolton Trust towards
the publication of this volume.
The publisher acknowledges the financial
assistance of the Scottish Arts Council.

A catalogue record for this volume is
available from the British Library.
ISBN 0-906772-95-8

Chapman New Writing Series
Editor Joy Hendry
ISSN 0953-5306

© Magi Gibson 2000
Magi Gibson is hereby identified as the author of
this work in accordance with Section 77 of the
Copyright, Design and Patents Act 1988.

Cover Illustration by Colin Dunbar

Some of the poems have appeared in the following magazines:
*Cutting Teeth, Deliberately Thirsty, The Stinging Fly, Krax,
Cencrastus, Spectrum, The Broadsheet, Chapman, West Coast
Magazine, Seam, Campus, The Herald* and *The Scotsman;* and in the
following anthologies: *Full Strength Angels, After the Watergaw,
Silent when I should be screaming,* and *Premier Results.* 'Bat Song'
and 'A Language That Knows No Words' appeared in *Strange Fish*
(Duende Poetry), a joint collection with Helen Lamb, 1997. 'Just Like
Eve' – poetry postcard – National Poetry Day 1999, 'Muse 3' appeared
in an earlier version in *Kicking Back* (Taranis Poetry). 'Weep Not for
Me' shortlisted in Scottish Open Poetry Competition 2000.

Printed by
Inglis Allen
Middlefield Road, Falkirk FK2 9AG

Contents

Forward

Anne MacLeod

The start of the third millennium is blessed by a resurgence in the world of Scottish poetry, and in particular a flourishing in Scottish women's poetry. The confidence of both poets and publishers is evident and growing. It is particularly pleasing, at this time to see Chapman Publishing, who have done so much fine work through the years, adding Magi Gibson to their flyte of poets. It has been too long since *Kicking Back* (Taranis 1993): and *Strange Fish* (Duende 1997) and *Premier Results* (Neruda 1997) served only to whet the appetite for this long-overdue collection.

Magi Gibson's career as poet and writer in residence is known to many throughout the length and breadth of Scotland. More than any other writer I know, she overcomes those borders of locality that so often define the Scottish wordsmith. Her work is known and appreciated from the Borders to the North-East, from Edinburgh's snell winds to Glasgow's rain. In *Wild Women of a Certain Age* she has produced a collection that will offer men and women in our culturally diverse nation much food for thought and her sometimes disturbing imagery will stir our deeper selves and strangely delight our senses.

Her deceptively gentle lyric style in no way diffuses deeply-held concerns, whether the anger be directed at a chauvinistic judge, our Scottish lack of political confidence, or the continued disempowerment of women. She is not afraid to use whatever tool seems most appropriate to a given theme; satire, humour, pathos are frequent in these pages, always carefully modulated. She is a poet who is not afraid of physical intensity. Much of the work is rich, sensual, steeped in reworked Celtic legend – the strong Queen Maeve a role-model in Janet Reger silk, burning the Celtic twilight in her fast red car. Gibson is much concerned with sensuality, with age, with allowed beauty – the social and aesthetic constraints that have been used to blunt, to control the female principle from Neolithic ages to the present day.

The voice here, as always in Magi Gibson's work, is soft and clear. She is a poet much concerned with clarity, with use of simple language; every syllable milked of its last drop of music in a poetry that is accessible, beguiling as a mountain stream. And yes, at times, wild.

The Female Poet on Reaching Forty

She's suddenly aware
of crow's feet marching round her eyes
of orange peel upon her thighs
and silver strands appearing in her hair.

She looks around
and is astounded
she is surrounded
by younger men.

And so she whispers to herself —
fuck forty then!

Wild Women of a Certain Age

My sisters, the time has come
to let your hair grow long and wild and grey,
to cast away the heated rollers and the tongs.

So when the moon is nine months full
let us meet out on our lawns,
let us burn our diet sheets,
let us pound our bathroom scales
to heaps of rusting springs.

Let us shred our measuring tapes,
our Firmer Buttocks videos.
Let us burn an effigy of Cher.
Let us tip our eye creams down the pan.
Let us revel in our pink plump ripeness.
Let us flaunt our stretch marks like shining honours.
Let us celebrate ourselves – because we can.

For we have bodies that have loved.
We have bodies that have lived.
Mouths that have savoured cheese and meat
and dribbled over chocolate and fruit,
tongues that have tasted good and evil,
lips that have sipped fine wines,
fingers that have stroked . . .

We have been the carriers of babes.
Our bellies have swollen with drumlin curves,
our breasts have hung like ripened fruit,
our teeth have bitten skin and threads.

We have swallowed bitter pills.
We have known dark bloodstains on our hands.
We have been the carriers of laughter and of pain,
the healers of our children's ills.
We have lain below the stars.
We have lain below our men.

Yes, sisters, now the time has come
to claim our bodies for ourselves.
For in our silver hair, our well-filled thighs,
in those laughter lines that crowd our eyes –
we live, we are alive.

What My Mother Told Me of My Birth

I was fathered by a grey sea mist that kissed
my mother's breasts and crept into her womb
while she gathered kail down on the shore.

Nine months gone, huge as a whale
she clambered slow and sore
up the steep flank of a mountain of pain
panting loud as Macha.

At the topmost peak, naked as daybreak
she sank down on a bed of jagged scree
and when her waters broke
a waterfall more beautiful
than the Grey Mare's Tail
gushed and tumbled to the blood-red sea.

The sun set and the moon rose high
while she writhed and thrashed,
her mountainous belly heaving
as granite and schist and gneiss once heaved
in the passion of creation.

Two days and two nights she struggled
with the devil's red-hot irons in her heart,
with stallions' hooves pounding at her skull,
with wolves' jaws tearing her apart.

Lightning sparked in thundery skies,
the wind howled like an unhallowed soul,
but always the moon watched over her –
a gentle mother with a fevered child.

Until the pain began to sink
as the sun sinks in the western sea
and a baby with gabbro eyes,
its lips as blue as glacier ice,
a caul upon its brow
grey as mist on a mountain top
slid from the fertile valley of her thighs.

Deirdre of the Sorrows

Well, I ask you
how would you have felt –
opening your eyes for the first time
staring from the cailleach's horny hands
and all around dolorous faces
girning and wailing
this child will bring the men of Ulster
nought but grief and sorrow?

It was a bit hard after that
to have a normal childhood.

Not that it was ever on the cards,
since the king, filthy old lecher,
decided there and then
he'd have me grown just big enough
(like a farmer waiting for a pink plump pig)
then stick me on the spit of his desires.

Oh, and of course, what a brilliant excuse –
since I was cursed, and only he
could break the geis –
if any other bedded me
it all would end in misery.

Childhood – lonely as an orphaned lamb
abandoned on a bleak hillside,
no-one but old Lebhorcham
to feed me tales
of Cuchulainn's daring-do
and what a curse I was
and how I should be grateful
that the King, brave man,
would save me from myself.

I ask you! Just because
they kept me isolated, uneducated.
Just because Nature blessed me
with a neck as slender as a swan's
eyes as blue as hyacinths
the grace of a doe in flight –
did they think I lacked intelligence?

Anyway, I spent my days (and sometimes nights)

running with the beasts of wood and hill.
I watched them birth and mate
and when at last I saw Noísiu riding by
his hair black as the raven's wing
his skin white as the mountain snow
his cheeks red as blood – I chose my fate.

Deirdre of the Sorrows, they call me.
Well, they always blame a woman if they can.
If life has taught me anything, it's that.
As far as I can see, the only thing
I could have changed
was not being born.

The Bog Girl's Tale

The first I knew was the dog howling
fit to split the moon in two.
Rough hands on my skin
hauling me from his crannog's warmth
to where a ring of fire
smudged the night with whorls of smoke.

They noosed a rope around my throat.
Such was my fright I wet myself.
Fetch water, the grey one cried,
she must be clean or else the god
will surely spit her back.

They shaved my head, one-half,
from milk-white brow to nape of neck,
cast raven fistfuls on the flames
adulteress adulteress adulteress
the flames whispered
and the women's eyes grew green and wide
as the eyes of toads
and their tongues hissed *adulteress*
and the moon shivered
and the skies began to weep
but I did not cry.

Then a silence
as though the sea herself
held still the breathing of the waves
as though the river ceased to flow
as though the wind had lost the will to rage . . .

They forced me to my knees,
led me tethered like a dog,
pushed me to the water's edge.
The black bog dragged me deep below.

But the dark god granted me the right to choose
what new form I should be – and I am
the roe deer running on the mountainside
I am the golden whin that sets the hill alight
I am the owl that haunts your midnight dream.

Yet all you see, as you file past this sealed glass chest
is matted hair, a shrivelled scrag of breast,
some scrapes of leathery skin stretched over bone,
a card that says – two thousand years ago
this woman met with death, outcast, alone.

Queen Maeve Addresses a Reluctant Lover

What do you fear in me, young man?
Did your mother tell you at her knee
of tortures suffered by Tam Linn?

Do you think that like the Faery Queen,
stripped of my Janet Reger silk,
my make-up and my anti-wrinkle cream,
I'll turn into a fierce cailleach
with winter in my hair and leathery skin?

Or have they told you old men's tales
of girls with teeth between their thighs
that chew – or worse still – bite?

Or is it that you fear
being sucked back in the womb
on a tidal wave of hot desire,
into that cave, that bowl of fire
where birth and life and death
dance and reel beneath a blood-red moon?

I am no hair-legged spider
no praying mantis beast
that would have my fun, then feast
upon your flesh.

I am no olive-skinned Delilah
who would shear your hair
and leave you feeble as a child.

Listen to the blood that beats
so hot and red and wild
within your breast.
Feel your hunger grow
much stronger than your fear.

Come now, my brave young man.
Come lie down here.

Queen Maeve Challenges the Men of Ireland

I am a fast red car
and will drive you to the edge
again and again

I am whisky on your ice –
I'll never slake your thirst
but man, I'll make your belly burn

I am a silver salmon
touch me with your tongue
taste the salt of my seven seas

I am a brothel window, all
lace and flesh and whispered fantasies

I am an apple tree –
after winter's cold
lie beneath my limbs –
when autumn frosts take hold
sink your teeth into my fruit's firm skin

I am the rounded moon
I can make you rage and swell
or calm you like a child

I am a pale pink shell –
run your finger round
the ridges of my whorl
hold me to your ear, hear
my secret oceans crash and roar

but most of all I'm fire –
linger by my crackling flame
warm yourself as I burn low
for soon, too soon you'll be no more
than a wisp of smoke, a smudge of ash
a half-remembered name

Queen Maeve Takes a Cab in Scotland

He drives the taxi, eyes firmly on the road
while her eyes explore the tattoo on his forearm –
a Saltire, and in white and blue – SCOTLAND FOREVER.

While she admires the way his thick black lashes curl,
the way his eyes shine blue as sapphires when he grins,
the firmness of his thighs beneath his jeans –
he tells her he loves Ireland (in his deep-voiced lowland lilt)
and adds, with innocent surprise – that Irish women love
a Scotsman on a Harley – in a kilt.

He's driving ever faster and
she's feeling ever hotter and
his meter's ticking fiercely
and she feels a strong attraction
and she's driven to distraction
almost at her destination.

Next time I call, she says as she slips some coins into his palm
and lets him feel the softness of her skin,
Forget the cab. Wear the kilt. Bring the Harley Davidson . . .

Queen Maeve Keeps Her Lover Late for Work

I regret I cannot let you leave my bed just yet.
For it occurs to me, even
in this dreamy state, there is perhaps a hair
somewhere on your arm I have not met.
Or a tiny mole, tucked away, maybe
in your inner thigh, up quite high,
or maybe on your neck?
And just behind your ear, yes, here,
a small birthmark – I'd like to memorise
just so I won't forget.

I regret if it's an inconvenience, sir,
to be kept here at my pleasure,
but I need to get the measure
to my satisfaction
of the pink perfection of your toes
and count each freckle on your chest and trace
the moonlines on your skin,
the sunlines on your face.

And then there is that tiny lilac bruise
just above the curve of your right shoulder.
And another just above your heel, I feel
I really need to kiss . . . again . . .

I Would Have Called It All a Dream

Last night my heart was cold and hard
as a well-turned cursing stone
as I lay, sleepless, by your side –
I might have been a hundred miles from you
I felt so alone.

And you slept sound as an old dog by the fire
and did not stir one hair, not when I sighed
a thousandth time, nor even when
he silently appeared and touched my arm
and led me from the loneliness
I was drowning in.

Outside he took me, past the barking dog,
out to the field, past dozing cows and sheep
to where the road runs straight, the drop is steep,
and boglands form the valley floor below.

But I saw no road and I saw no bog –
instead a cold sea filled the land
as they say it did a million years ago,
and my toes sank deep in soft, damp sand
and the full moon cast her silver wand
across the ink-black flow.

So cold I was from fright and lack of sleep
I hardly felt the water's icy tongue
as it licked my feet then lapped my legs.
I took his hand and swam out from the shore
until the moon and stars grew blurred.
I dived behind him to the ocean bed
and swear that on his head he wore
a silken cap of red.

I was happy there, where time's insistent metronome
is silenced by the dolphins' haunting song.
And I would have stayed,
making love or combing out my hair
or stitching gloves from delicate fishscales
had he not said seven years had passed
and I must go home.

Anyway, I tip-toed in
before the small birds stirred the leaves
to prattle at the dawn.
I slipped so gently down
beside your sleeping form
you did not stir. I lay and listened
to the lorries rumble on the road
and would have called it all a dream
but for the footprints damp with sand
that trail from the front door to our room
the glistening scales still clinging to my hand
and the child with oceans in his eyes
now swimming in my womb.

Shela-na-gig

Splay-thighed moon-belly sister
you stare defiance
with your four wide eyes
you grin wild mischief
with your two broad smiles
you dare mild-mannered men
and lady-labelled women
to hold your brazen gaze.

How much I long to be like you!
Naked and true, never hiding
your lustful light below
the bushel of false modesty.

How many curious eyes have dropped
their lids before your honesty?
How many more have stopped to stare
and wonder what unhallowed hands would dare
to sculpt you from cold stone?

They tried to kill you once,
called you shameless, harlot, whore
burned you with their righteous indignation
drowned you for the open invitation
you give for fun and fornication.

Perhaps they feared your bold reminder –
we are born of women, are not gods.

Shela-na-gig – old lady who squats
La Que Saba, weathered by centuries
of storm and scorn –

when the moon is full
and the stars are birling wildly in the sky
do you leap around our winter fields
running with the old grey wolves
baubo belly dancing
so Demeter will laugh again
and raise Persephone
from the underworld's dark tomb?

Baubo – Greek goddess of obscenity with nipples for eyes, and a vulva for a mouth. She appeared to Demeter in her grief and so amused her that Demeter's spirits were raised and she set off to rescue Persephone

Liffey Dreams

Outside our hotel room
the Liffey waters roll, thick as treacle,
dark as the blood of Kerry witches,
black as Cromwell's soul.

It's 2 am
a man is screaming
and I can't tell if he's calling out
from pleasure or from pain.

A shout. A crash of glass. Feet running.
A siren wailing, insistent as
a wakeful child, looping fear into the dark.

Through all this dreams come –
dreams of a baby born to a girl
I saw last night, shivering
in O'Connell street.

Dreams of a baby wrapped in a rag
swimming its way down to the sea
under O'Connell Bridge
in dark Liffey water,
past the thin family frozen in bronze
and the mangy mongrel
whimpering at their heels.

Even with her eyes downcast
even in her misery
and her hunger and her pain
as she treads forever Destitution Road
the thin mother sees
the drowned baby swimming
wide-eyed as a seal pup
and mizzling tears stream down her face.

It's 8 am
propped against cloud pillows
I watch far traffic as it flows
a relentless river of rubber and metal
over O'Connell Bridge.

Grey sky, grey wind, grey rain, grey day
a world of monochrome
and one bright red van.

Shaman of the Elements

A flood fierce enough to sweep a town away,
a sea of tranquillity to float dreams on

you make Earth blue, grass green
and when you tumble from

the pitcher of the sky, the darkness gleams
with a trillion silver arrowheads in flight.

Shaman of the elements –
you freeze the eyelash of the Inuit to white,

you wet the worker in the paddy field,
you caul the mountains with your mist

the beauty of your dew upon a spider's web
or on a quivering leaf
makes poets lift their pens to write.

Shape-shifter – wake me from my dreams
with water which once graced a glacier in Tibet.

Christen the infant at the font with snowflakes
that once melted on the Hudson or the Seine.

Quench my thirst with drops which glistened
on a Pharaoh's brow, or in a brickie's sweat.

Sweet water – ancient salt-tongued sculptor,
whose tides define the edges of our lands,

whose strength has crumbled cliffs to grains of sand,
fall gently on my upturned face,

seduce me with your finger's pattering dance,
share with me a lover's last embrace.

Water, Wasser, Uisge, Eau and a million unknown names –
slumbering in a reed-fringed loch, you are
a shining mirror for the universe

shimmering as a rainbow in the sky, you stir
the pagan in my soul –

from deserts and sickbeds the dying call for you,
in a thousand tongues the drowning curse your power.

Show mercy when I'm waving to the shore –
let the boatman row me safely over.

Winter Solace

That night she wandered the city cold
looking for a sign – a shooting star,
a diamond in the road.

She met him in a bar, shivering
under threadbare layers of loneliness.
Sitting on a stool she wandered with him

down the dead-ends of his life.
Around them laughter burst like champagne fizz,
dark city rhythms knifed the neon night.

He said *please take me home.*

Before the blue hiss of her fire
she peeled the sadness from him –
black coat, black shirt, black shoes.

She knelt like Mary Magdalene
and with warm kisses washed his feet
then dried them with her hair.

I don't want to sleep with you
he said, his voice still cold
from centuries of living in a glacier.

*But let me lie beside your warmth –
just once, just for tonight.
I need someone to hold.*

A host of voices – mother, father, friends –
urged her to say no. Doubt chilled her
for a moment like a ghost.

Under a soft white duvet cloud
she sucked the wound the world had gouged
into his soul until he bled no more.

She held him close, and as the nightdark died
and dawnlight stroked their skin, he melted in
to her through every nerve and pore.

In the morning when she woke
she found him gone, the white shroud
of his dreams an empty tangle by her side.

When You Step from the Shower

When you step from the shower
it's as though you've stepped from some ancient forest
raindrops shimmering in your hair like jewels

When you step from the shower
you sparkle as though the stars have fallen from the sky
and rested on your skin

I want to kiss you then, run my tongue
along the rivers of your arms

But you walk round the room
not knowing the beauty of your every move
not knowing how I want to smooth the golden hair
that curls still damp upon your breast

You glow warm as the morning sun
that makes the small flower turn its head,
spread its crimson petals wide

And when you bend
your spine describes a pattern
intricate as tiny sea-shells shifting
beneath your topaz skin

You come from the shower
tempting as a tight-skinned fruit
glistening with early morning dew

I love your nakedness, the man in you
that melts the space between my hips.

I love to watch you dress, but not just yet, my love –
the shirt, the socks, the bus, the boss must wait –
first let me have just one small kiss . . .

Baby We Were Born for This

I'm driving fast and furious
as a harpy from hell
Bruce Springsteen's in my passenger seat
belting baby we were *Born to Run*
so I roll down the window

let the wind blow back my hair
and in my rear-view mirror
the road's a dark green tunnel
while up ahead
the white line's got it all stitched up.

Then Brucey says
I've got a *Hungry Heart*,
let's stop off in Macduff

eat fish suppers on the rocks
then make love
where the sea comes crashing in
and I cave in without a fight
cos I see his jeans so fine and tight
and smell his leather jerkin
and I need an *Everlasting Kiss*
to quell the fire that's raging.

So we breeze into Macduff
past kids that haunt the shadows
of graffitied harbour walls
and with the suppers and Irn Bru
we drive to where the sea falls
into an endless dream of darkening blue
and *I just can't see
what a guy like him is doing with me*
on this wind-blown north-east shore
cos I ain't that young anymore

but he says, hey babe, it's all right
*show a little faith
there's magic in the night*
stars riding the highway of the sky
seagulls surfing the oil-black tide
the wind stroking the world's pain
and my *Secret Garden* opens wide

and I want to tell him oh so much
there's healing in his *Human Touch*
and it ain't no sin, it ain't no sin
I'm glad to be alive.

In the lonely cool before the dawn
I pull the tartan rug around
the strong curve of his shoulder.
I stare up at the stars that yawn,
brush his eyelids with a kiss
and whisper, Brucey, baby,
we were born for this.

The Day the Elfin Queen Met Tom of Ercildoune

I'm driving from the supermarket
or maybe it's from the office
and this is in Glasgow or
it might be Inverness
and you're standing there
like a bewildered deer beside the road,
or a fledgling fallen from the nest,
in your hand the photo of a child,
in your eyes a brooding loneliness.

And I stop (and pay no heed
to the small voice nipping at my ear
to put the foot down and drive on).

You climb in and off we speed
and my car becomes a fine white steed.
I, the Fairy Queen, foxy in a red silk dress,
you, young Tom of Ercildoune
with fires in your brown eyes
that melt my hips to mead.

Each time I change from second into third
my left hand brushes your right thigh
while from the radio
a voice drifts cool and soft
as snowflakes from a winter sky

Tell me where you want to go
Take a breath when I ask you to
Just try . . .

Close your eyes, I'll take you there
I could take you anywhere
Come fly . . .

And I inhale the wisps of smoke
which moments before explored your mouth
and I envy the cigarette that knows
the velvet of your lips.

I wish I could grow feathered wings.
I'd fly into your arms
as a small bird flies into the lush
green branches of a tree.

I'd slip my fingertips
along your smooth pale bark
to where the lichen grows
to where the dark root sleeps.

Small, hungry bird –
I'd steal from your young tree
its star-bright seed.
I'd satisfy my own hot greed.

Suddenly a red light flares.
My foot hits the brake.

Or was it daylight's fingers
cold and bony as a crone's
tugging at the night-time sky
that startled us awake?

We travelled that sweet road for hours,
or maybe it was years
for we had time to talk of books and films,
of poetry, plays and politics,
of the child smiling your smile
in a country far away
yet never did we speak of loneliness
the icy star
the twisted thorn
the small, sharp stone.

These days, my young and beautiful,
my bold, straight-talking man,
I drive alone through sleet that slants
like sharpened arrowheads,
my fine white stallion gone,
my clothes plain,
my hair grey as the mountain mist,
my heart caught fast
in the Cailleach's fist.

The Truth about Tam Linn

There was no rowan planted at your gate
and it was your hand that opened it
your smile that welcomed me
your voice that asked me in.

Did you not see the warning signs?
The way my black hair loosened

from its tightly tied-back bun
into noose-like coils, into loaded springs?

How could you have missed
the triple purple irises,
the green glow from my eyes?

Not even when I took my jerkin off
and hung it on a moonbeam
did you express surprise
or recall tales your mother told
of fairy women who would kiss your lips
then suck the marrow from your soul.

You, with your peat brown eyes
and your king-size bed
its silken sheets drawn back
in cool anticipation, in open invitation
and your tapestries of courtiers and courtesans
gazing down from scenes of coy seduction.

O.K. So I had swapped my snow-white steed
for a Harley Davidson,
my robes of shimmering green and gold
for blackest leather and blue denim.

But my bright-eyed boy
with the hunger in your groin
and the fever on your brow
don't ever claim you didn't know the score
when you placed your lips on mine
cool as water from a shaded glen,
when you let your hands explore
the heaths and mountains of my realm.

Don't claim it was a spell I cast
a fairy arrow in your ear
or hemlock slipped into your wine.

You bounded to my arms,
eager as the cock runs to the hen.

You weren't pushed or pulled,
but like a silver moth that flies towards the moon,
like a salmon seeking out the stony womb,
you made your way alone, Tam Linn,
you gladly rushed right in.

Reading in Bed

afterwards he sleeps
limbs spread on crumpled sheets
air dark with summer heat

a hieroglyph
of hair, skin, muscle, bone

her fingers read
for pleasure

Sometimes I Dream

Sometimes I dream
of the tin soldier with the one leg

and in my dream I want to be
the pretty ballerina
(he loves so much)
with the skin of softest peach
and the pretty cherry pout he
wants to kiss, and I want to dress
in frilly, frothy, strawberry frocks
and spend my days
twirling in a tinkling music box.

But I know, deep down, I am the fish –
the brown trout leaping in a Scottish loch
scales shimmering in pale November sun

and always in my dream
I open up and swallow down
the soldier's cold, thin form.

Inside me he struggles,
kicks with his one good leg –
and I cannot dream on

because no-one
not even a plain brown trout
in a cold grey loch

wants to feel the metal
hook her tongue
the line whip and reel her in
the marble slab
the knife's cold cut

just so the hero
can get out.

Blessed Be

Blessed be the long black dress
for it hides a multitude of sins

Blessed be candlelight
for it casts a mellow glow –
is kind to older skins

Blessed be the wonderbra
for it maketh our cups to overflow

Blessed be Camilla Parker Bowles
for next to her
we are all beautiful as princesses

Blessed be Maggie Thatcher
for next to her
we are all Angels of Mercy

Blessed be our hairdressers
for they fill our greying world with colour

Blessed be the mirror
in the ladies in Est Est Est
for it makes even the fattest
(who will always be with us)
thin

But so much more than all of these,
oh blessed be St Michael –
for he gives us shaper-tights
and fresh cream cakes in a one-stop-store.

Wild Woman Rap

I'm a bodybag of bones
I'm a bucketful of blood
grown from a rib
moulded from mud
I've feet made of clay
and the brain of a bird
my head's in the clouds
and my heart's on the wing
I've a hole in my soul
where the pain gets in

I'm a mother's only daughter
I'm nobody's child
the world thinks it's tamed me
but my spirit runs wild
I've been ground down to dust
I've been pillared to salt
I ate the wormy apple – the fall was all my fault
I'm young and I'm old
sizes six to eighteen
there's a hole in my soul
where the pain gets in

I'm an angel who can bless
I'm a black-hearted witch
I'm a sister of mercy
I'm a man-stealing bitch

I'm a mother – I'm a daughter
I'm a mistress – I'm a wife
I've passion in my thighs
makes for trouble and strife
I'm a pillow for your sadness
I'm a six to your nine
with a hole in my soul
where the pain gets in

I'm a slave girl – I'm a peasant,
I'm a princess – I'm a queen
I'm old and I'm young
I'm generous and I'm mean
lust's a ruby in my belly
truth's a diamond on my tongue
I've milk in my breasts
I've a child in my womb
and a hole in my soul
where the pain gets in

Poems to the Muse

1

I give birth to this poem.
It's my easiest labour yet.
I'm still on my feet,
still walking around.

No more than a dull ache
low in my groin.

Now it slides from me
wet and slippery little fish,
slips easy onto this white sheet,
stretches its perfect vowels,
kicks its tiny consonants.

I cut its cord with my teeth,
clean it with my tongue,
hold it out for you to take.

You planted the seed.
Without you it would not be.
Cradle it in your arms.
Hold it close

as it gulps the moist air
and fills its lungs
and calls your name.

2

When you first appeared
uninvited
deep inside my head
I thought you were the dark man
every women's said
to have inside – an unmet love – a fantasy
some kind of ghost
to keep me company
on lonely nights.

I could have lived quite comfortably
with a dark and handsome ghost.

It is the reality of you
that scares me so.

3

Please come round tonight. I really want
to see you. But don't be embarrassed when
I ask you to take off your clothes

outside the door, to lift from your head
that unattractive hat – it shades the tears
and laughter in your eyes – to cast away

that coat of twitching anxiety,
(by all means leave it worrying at the door
for your safe return). And that stick

you like to carry to beat yourself
to a misery, lose it on the way or
at the very least, leave it lying lifeless

on the front porch floor. Please
come round tonight. I want so much
to see you as you really are.

4

I was a deserted house
doors locked against the world
within my walls, tables, chairs, beds
were wrapped in dustsheet shrouds.
Even the spiders had packed up and left.

Then I glimpsed you
passing quickly in a crowd
and my heart leapt
somersaulted into life
sunlight flooded my darkened rooms
inside my head blood pumped fierce
– my own breath stirred the shrouds.

The Muse's Reply

Can't you see I'm all surface?
I smile when you smile
flick back my hair when you laugh
mimic your every mood.

So, I have a face you could love?
You could drown yourself
in the deep blue of my eyes?
I am your idea of paradise?

Without you I am nothing.
I am an illusion
a grain of gravel can distort,
a darting fish can shatter.

At the first whisper of wind
at the first grumble of thunder
at the first raindropteardrop
pattering the surface of this water

I'll disappear
leaving you alone
gazing at nothingness.

Scotland oh Scotland

My poor small country
struggling under the weight
of so much calvinistic decency!

Scared to make love
with passion and nakedness
lest your civilised neighbours
twitch at their border curtains
and call you savages.

You chase tartan rainbows
waving lucky plastic heather,
you search for tea-leaves at the bottom
of a thousand whisky bottles
to convince yourself
there is a future.

While somewhere deep below
an outward show
of growing confidence
of MSPs and Scottish Parliament,
your underbelly churns and growls;
your prisons overflow
with suicides and wasted lives,
your kids kick burst dreams
at ever-moving goalposts
on graffiti-splattered housing schemes,
and your old folk freeze
alone
watching *Win A Million*
on rented TV screens.

And still – to trawl those tourists in,
those silver-dollar-darlings,
you package up your sense of nationhood
in shortbread tins, in haggis skins,
in cozy tartan rugs, in highland toffee bars,
in football teams, in bull-necked rugby stars –

while behind this pseudo-culture kitsch and keech
you try to hide the awful truth
that no-one dares to utter –

you are the lion rampant
that whimpers
and never ventures from its den –

the David that never leaves his bed
to face Goliath with his stone and sling –

beaten before you begin,
a purple-faced thistle full of pricks
in ginger wigs and tartan tammies
crying

F-R-E-E-D-O-M

in cinemas and city streets and pubs
crying
in your nightmares for your mammies.

Oh my sad, sad people
who think that Demo Crassi
is the latest Baywatch Bimbo,
who sit in living rooms and lounges
staring at Sky
while your seas are poisoned,
your food is modified
your intellect is stultified –

and in your towns and villages
your kids go chasing dragons
and their young dreams die –

how dare you have the brass effrontery
to say you're on the way
to self-determination

How dare you have the gall
to claim your re-birth as a nation?

Weep Not for Me

The Scottish Act Anent Child Murder of 1690 stated that any woman who concealed pregnancy, called for no help at birth, and whose child was dead or missing, was to be hanged. There were 347 indictments and investigations for infanticide between 1690 and 1800.

1

I was a tight closed bud at springtime;
he touched me and I opened
in the warmth of his smile I uncurled
moist petals of desire.

Reflected in his peat-brown eyes
on the high moor heather,
the thyme-scent heavy on the air,
I saw rainbows and stars and skies
and endless possibilities.

I saw Adam and Eve in Paradise.

2

Not sudden, not like at a cliff's edge
with a steep drop to
rocks and sea below, but a low
dream slide, hair flowing like a swimmer's
on gentle waves of air, petticoats billowing
white cotton-grass clouds – a gentle glide

as if at any point I could wake, grasp a jut of rock,
a tuft of heather, or his strong hand
to pull me back.

Not sudden, but a slow sinking
a strange dream, a sorrowful awakening.

3

Wrested from the spell he cast
with his hot and hungry touch
my eyes open, my breasts fill, my waist thickens.

By the oak tree I wait, by the dark gate I wait
by the stream's edge I wait, my breasts fill
my waist thickens, the sky darkens.

Around my feet ferns uncurl, deadly nightshade
nods her bonnet head, toadstools' white flesh beckons
the air darkens, my breasts fill, my waist thickens.

Deep inside me fear stirs, the dark thickens
my heart sickens, the child quickens
turns uneasy in its dream

4

Tight-tied, dry-eyed, I clean and set the grate,
scour the flags, milk the cows, lay out the linen
on the grass, fetch the peats, curtsey when the master
passes by, but
when the moon drags, I cut
myself, wash the bloodied rags, play the cursed charade,
bide my nine-month time, stifle my midnight sobs
suffocate my unborn dreams, whisper
to the heartbeat in my breast,
the heartbeat in my womb
he loves me, he loves me not
knowing in my soul he will not come

5

If our union was Paradise then this is Hell.

Alone in black woods, ferns reach out, thorns
rip flesh, cold boulder pillow, damp earth
birthing bed, bruised berries burst blood seed
pain bleed earth black stained stars leering
fox reek, vomit stench, writhing in pain
writhing in shame, owl calls
banshee screams
    I
       give birth
           to ruin

6

First their eyes
sharp as the eyes
of the blackbird
that see the worm
below the grass.

Then their tongues
sharp as the claws
of the cat
that strike
in midnight dark.

7
She squeezed my breasts
her gnarled hand
cold and white
against the swollen
blue-veined pink.

Milk, sour
as week-old butter,
oozed yellow as sin

8
no bigger than a rabbit
hung in the byre
curled like a springtime fern
tight into itself, blue
as a blaeberry cold in my arms

cold in my arms

moonlight ghouled its face
silvered its staring eyes, hooked
the breath from its gasping mouth

it never cried
it never cried

9
The boulder, bigger
than the rabbit child.

A hand not mine, a mother's hand, a
monster's hand raised
to the shoulder

caught in that moment

forever, in that moment
lives, forever, in that moment
dies

10
Weep not for me – I'll gladly hang
my sorrow on your gallows tree.

Weep not for me –
death's the only hope I have
to set me free.

Weep not for me
I am not worthy of your tears.

What Drives Me, You Ask

as if I'm a juggernaut
with a hairy-armed trucker at my wheel
or a shiny car or train
bolting through the landscape
of my life.

Perhaps the wind drives me, I say,
as it drives the sleet and snow
that sting and numb the senses.

But no! I am driven
by the fire that rages in my head
when I see a wife beaten
a child branded evil
a junkie with a paper cup
a woman in a blaze of kerosene
a child with fag burns on her feet
with ropemarks on her neck
with bruises on her thighs
with pain in her heart.

I am driven to violence
against my typewriter.

I plead guilty
to battering its pale keys
to bruising the blank indifference
of a thousand sheets of paper.

I am driven by a driver without a licence.

I am driven by the ordinary
madness of existence.

Drifter

She nibbled at life,
could not quite take it
in bite-size pieces.

Some say it started when
she refused the nipple,
lay in her mother's arms
stiff and cold as a piece of wood.

Others said no – the mother
was dry and wizened,
her scant milk too sour.
The bairn had nuzzled,
had known a bitter suckling.

Either way, it did the child no good.

She carved her body,
cut into its smooth bark,
to prove what?

that she could/could not feel?
could/could not be hurt?
that the sap would pulse warm and red
that she too was flesh and blood?

Fourteen years old, she cut free
on a new moon and a spring tide.
She floated like driftwood
to dark, cruel shores.
Even the salt of life's sea

could not wash her wounds clean.

Goldilocks

She wakes beside a man
with greying stubble on his chin.
She notes how the muscles on the arm
hauled heavily across her breasts
feel no longer young, no longer firm,
how on his neck the thin pale flesh
crinkles like boiled milk skin.

She calculates his age
as if he was a tree
she'd sliced through
and could count the rings.

Old enough to be her father –
that makes her smile, snuggle closer.

She shuts her eyes
but does not dream.
This bed is warm,
a sheltered lair
she has burrowed into.
It smells of him
of sweat, of stale cologne
of last night's beer
of big strong daddy bear.

In the scullery she rummages
for cereal, milk, a bowl
turns the radio low
lights a fag, finds a comb
runs its blunt teeth through her hair,
makes herself at home.

no angel

After Judge Ian Starforth Hill described a nine year old rape victim as "not exactly an angel herself" and gave her attacker two years' probation.

she was nine and half her milk teeth
gone because she'd kissed the boys
behind the shed And she listened in
on big girl/bad girl jokes and laughed and
laughed until she wet her knickers though
she never understood what was so funny she
was only nine but already knew the ins and
outs of Sexual Intercourse They'd done it in
class with Miss Jones And she'd seen it
on the telly a million times though she
never looked not really just pretended while
she counted the leaves on the weeping fig
and she might well have known a con
dom if she'd met one in the street And it cannot
be denied she'd played kiss/kick/torture and
enjoyed it And snogged Jamie from the High
School for ten minutes under the chute without
taking
a
breath
with three independent witnesses so it
shouldn't have surprised you not really when
her past was revealed in court and the Judge
with all the Wisdom of his Wig the Judge
with all the Gravity of his Gown
revealed that the victim the
nine year old victim
of the sex attack

was no angel

Kate

Kate, strapped in her machine chair
speaks to us *plip – plip – plip*
says she likes ballroom dancing
but this room is too small
and her battery is low.

Today, indoors, she's dressed
in woollen mitts, her head lolls
like a knitted doll, her earrings dangle,
her legs foetus-curl as her headset dances,
pecks its long slim beak like an exotic bird
at the computer board.

She listens like a CIA man –
nothing sneaks past her brain,
more agile than ours.
It performs double flips
listening while her headset
pecks words that wriggle on the air
for us to catch.

Suddenly she takes us by surprise
YOU   *plip*
ARE   *plip*
A   *plip*
CHEEKY   *plip*
BITCH   *plip*
and a cocked head grin.

Kate is proud of her vocabulary range.
It took her hours to programme
all the swear words in.

A Language That Knows No Words

Xavier slouches at the front, slices
shavings from a pencil with an open blade.
I stand before a blackboard I cannot reach
because Xavier ripped out the wood dais
two teachers ago.

Karim, tall and dark and beautiful, smiles.
I speak English, he says
in an American Movie Accent,
I love you, baby, he says
while Xavier's blade slices
slices in a language that knows no words.

I point to the radio on the floor.
Who can plug this in, I ask.
Radia laughs, a knowing laugh.
A women at fourteen, hair henna-ed red, mother
a whore. You pretty, says Radia.
You make good prostitute.
I point to the radio, she points to the wall.
Wires ragged as severed nerves jut
from a jagged hole. Xavier, she says
and shrugs. And Xavier stretches
like a cat and his eyes shine
shine like the blade of his knife.

Later I see the Directrice. She gives me
coffee and five minutes and half an ear.
She strokes her poodle, feeds it sugar,
says she is a very busy woman.

In my room the air hangs still and sour.
Xavier's pencil is no more. On his desk
wood slivers darken, shrivel, curl.

The schoolbell rings, the students shriek
like startled jungle birds towards the door
but Xavier remains.

Still as a cat about to pounce
he stares into my eyes,
then cups the shavings in his hands
and softly softly blows
the small brown curling feathers
to the floor.

Three Poems for a Lost Boy

Rather than . . .

Rather than this slow wasting
I'd choose for you some ancient initiation
into the realm of manhood.

Rather than those adolescent eyes
shadowed from tedious hours
staring at telly and computer screen
I'd smudge your eyes with woad,
shove you out into the wilderness,
have you start life's journey,
not with a UB40 and a clutch of grades,
not with a thin portfolio of failure,
not firing off an endless trail of envelopes
filled with skeletal CVs,
not hunting a scattering of vacancies – no

I'd send you with a wand of willow in your fist –
I'd have you fire a hail of sharpened arrows,
I'd have you hunt the eagle, track the hare,
I'd have you climb high mountains,
not of setbacks/cutbacks/drawbacks/knockbacks
New Deals/RawDeals/No Deals
but of schist and granite –
I'd have you go climb mountains
just because they're there.

Poem for a Lost Boy

I crept into your room tonight
about eleven o'clock, just as I used to do
when you were eight or nine years old.

But you were gone –
it came as quite a shock to find
your bed so empty, cold.

Since then I've tried to recollect

the moment when you left –
while I chatted at the shops?
or maybe as I couch-potato slouched
staring at the world's disasters?

Your room was tidy, the Lego neatly
stored below the bed in two red
plastic boxes, your cars
precision-parked along the windowsills.

Your books and tapes and videos
lined the shelves, dusty with memories.
Photos of you smiled down from the walls –
a small blonde boy, eyes shining.

And then I realised I hadn't seen
that child for such a long dark time.

So, when I crept into your room
expecting his blonde and tousled head
dreaming on the pillow, expecting
to kiss his sleep-warm cheek
it frightened me to find him gone.

Tonight I'll leave a window open –
just in case. I'll leave
the door unlocked,
the stair light on.

To a Boy Who Thinks He Has Somehow Failed

I never wanted you to be Prime Minister,
your eyes glistening with shallowness,
your tongue silver-tipped and treacherous.

I never wanted you to be a soldier
spilling blood on foreign soil,
your flesh and bones fodder
for the summer grass.

When you lay there wide-eyed in the cradle of my arms
I never wished for you the champion's lot,
I never wanted medals or a sideboard bristling trophies –
shiny tokens of . . . what?

I never wanted you to be a teacher/lawyer/sailor/spy/
a penny-pushing banker/a wan pen-pushing wanker/
a managing director/grease monkey/pig or screw.

I never wanted you to be anything
but you.

An Open Letter to the Mother of the Three Little Pigs

I wonder if they swore at you, cursed you
as an old mean sow, when you packed their bags
and barred your door?

Did you fret when rumours filtered through
the wolf was on their patch?

How did you dampen down your mother love
and stop yourself from rushing round
to scratch that old wolf's eyes clean out?
And when you heard the youngest child
who'd always caused you so much grief –
those school reports – *a wide-eyed dreamer,*
lazy, could do better. Remember
all his wild nightmares? When you heard he'd built
a flimsy house of straw, what held you back
from trotting round to fetch him home?

And the second, with his house of sticks
and so much fire about. Okay, so
there were plenty wagging tongues
who said he was no good –
too busy chasing sows to bide
at home and make his four walls strong –
BUT YOU WERE HIS MOTHER!

How did you feel when news came through
he'd met a cruel death?

And the third – is it true
he always was your piggish pride and joy,
your pink-skinned, blue-eyed boy?

Tell me, Mrs Mother Pig, how often does he call?

And does he say, well, mother,
now you're getting old and frail,
don't fret, do come and bide
within my fine brick walls?

Dear Mrs Pig, you understand
I ask these questions
only because
as the mother of three young sons
I am quite curious.

Bat Song

So, our features offend
you. Too shrunken-
skulled, too rat-eyed,
ugly web-winged embryos.

Skinny in leather and slinky
fur, do you find our forms
too nazi for your
civilised sensibilities?

You blame the moon
for our presence.

But we have always been/are
always here –

armies of us sleeping
in your soulless churches,
fornicating in the rafters,
pissing on prayerbooks and pews.

Or lurking in dark dank
places your kind once too
inhabited.

We stream at dusk like smoke
into your streets, scribe
the thin black air with
strange graffiti.

You claim we make your
flesh crawl, appearing
out of darkness and silence.

Is it our fault, Sir,
that you are deaf
to the beauty of our songs?

I Learn to Talk Their Language

In here it's black,
        silence fills
my mouth like fur.   There is not

light,   but the door
  they pushed me through is

defined
  by a thin line of light

and is a lie they
told me.

This is a door, they said, but it
    is not.
You can open a door. You can shut

a door. But this door does not
              open
for me

and through its solidness
          sounds
slither and
   even with the fur
           thick on my tongue
my mouth weeps tears,
           its small pink pores
like flowerbuds opening,
like berries   bursting.

      From time to time they feed me words.
These words will make you, make you well,
they say
     slipping the words through their teeth, through
       clenched teeth I try to
grasp
       each word, each

slippy little lizard

   hold its frightened body in my mouth

feel its heartbeat pound
   its meaning pulse, but

do not want to gulp it down . . .

                                                              eat it . . .

                                      kill   it . . .

And I shrink deep
          back to where the silence wraps
around me like a thick black fur.

They wait outside, the white

light crackles.   I cower
          – they force live, words between my lips,   raw
words I want, I hunger for, but

do not want to swallow, not want to
kill –   I beg them with
               the roundness of my eyes –
no more – no more,
                  but now I see the door

is not a door,   it is a gaping
             purple mouth
             and through its lips
sounds flutter,   soar
and the black fur shrivels
          as the language splits,
                  spills,
                        falls like splintering
stars
blinding bright against the black

                       I pick them up, piece
syllables like   shards of shattered cups   until they

hold their meanings once again   like cups hold water, milk

I lift them to my lips, gulp colours, tastes, life death, laughter
tears . . .

Now each day I leave the silent dark
and hunt fresh wriggling words,

I tear my fingernails as they scurry off like rats
I spear them with my tongue, I catch their tails,

crunch sharpened teeth on brittle consonants,
I strip their skins, suck marrow from their vowels,
spit out the gristle of their syllables.

    I thread their whitened bones on silver skin.

The Silence of Women

In this room we see
exhibited inside glass
a collar made of iron,
its girth the handspan
of a woman's throat.
The words she could not speak
trapped on its sharpened spike
for three centuries.

In an isolation cell
a woman screams
screaming till the screams
fill up the space
like water filling up a well.
She is drowning
in the silence she is drowning
in the sound of screams.

In a dilapidated flat
wallpaper strips
hang from the walls
like tongues.
It's Friday night. She smells
his beery breath. She feels
his boot, his fist. Her mouth
fills up with blood.

Her sobs are silent.

Game, Set and Match

A squash ball, she calmly said
smashing each word
at the white wall of anger

they'd built between them,
is dark, small, hard, cold.
You want to play, she said,

you beat it, hit it, bounce it
off the floor, the wall . . .
You snort and grunt and sweat

Then cup it gently in your fist
pleased at its warm softness
pleased it's ready now to play your game.

I am small and dark, she said softly,
serving the words at the crumbling wall.
You find me hard and cold, she said,

lobbing each word, watching it fall,
but never try to warm me up with shows of force –
I'll not come bouncing back to play your game
or share your bed.

Personal and Social Development

We had sex today
Period 3, with Miss Sprott.

We covered all the big stuff first – got
gonorrhoea, herpes, crabs

then we saw some overheads
of the sexual organs

and Miss Sprott spluttered
about IUDs and Dutch Caps

and Eilidh said she'd always thought
they were magic mushrooms

and *Miss*, she asked, *is a sixty-nine
sex with a smallish ice cream and a flake?*

and Miss Sprott burnt bright scarlet
and said we'd better stick to the bare
essentials of the topic.

The bit with the condom
and the cucumber

and the suicidal cream
was a real giggle.

The rest was a bit of a drag
which Miss Sprott said it all was anyway –

vastly over-rated, she insisted
and Eilidh whispered
Like she'd know!

Afterwards me and Eilidh couldn't wait
to rush behind the bike sheds
for a fag.

Next week we're doing childbirth.

Poem for My Sister

We hang in an island of sea,
our wildness trapped inside our father's lens,
held captive all these years within a plain black frame.
Summer, sixty-three or four and we forever
younger than our own offspring.

Friends grin to see us on my kitchen wall –
you so blond, me so dark, yet sisters still.

Despite the photo's grainy black and white
the yellow of my silk swimsuit sings out,
the turquoise of yours glistens. My face
is shaded by salt-tousled hair.

You, laughing, splash cold water
on my thin brown legs, while I dash
deeper in the darkening waves.

Dead man's fingers, seaslugs, devilfish,
slimy, swaying, bladderwrack.

what unseen monsters might have lurked
around us as we laughed and larked?

Remember what the old men said –
the sea glows in the dark.

Treasure, my sister, this fading photograph.
Treasure the innocence we had
before the sickness grew within our blood.
Treasure the unscarred beauty of our skins
before they knew the surgeon's blade.

Go back some day, wade out
until the water splashes at your knees –
you'll hear our childish laughter once again,
echoing, echoing in the breeze.

Peachy Paterson

Peachy Paterson jumped me
up the High Line
tried to bring me doon
screamin oan and oan
that Ah wis a stuck-up bitch
jist cos eftir last week's dance
Ah widnae let him walk me home.

Big Karla's dad wiz German –
she wiz built like a Panzer Tank.
She flicked him off
like he wiz an irritatin midge
an he landed in the ditch.

Ah ran away
near peein ma knickers
him bellowin at ma back
Ah widnae touch ye if ye paid me
ya poxy hoor-faced bitch.

Planting Crocuses with My Mother

While I dug out the holes
she tipped out the bulbs,
little brown and papery hearts
playing dead beside the granite headstone
on my father's grave.

She popped the nuggets in
her fingers stiffening with cold,
the knuckles swollen-boned and red.
Then we replaced each sod,
patted back the damp October grass
until it looked as if we'd never been.

There should be a fine show in spring,
she said. *Even better the year after.*
We stood and stared as if to visualise
the tiny yellow, white and lilac heads
stretching thin green necks
towards bright April skies.

Then again, she laughed, rubbing her hands
to make them warm. *If I go soon,*
you'll have to dig the whole lot up again.

Auld Claes and Porritch

Don't pick the flowers
you always said when I was small
it's such a waste
they last much longer in the ground

Keep good clothes good – I hung around
in seconds, slightly soileds,
in fire-sale clothes and hand-me-downs,
waiting for High Days and Holidays
and Flying Pigs and Blue Moons
so I could get the chance
to choose the pretty pinafore,
to don the frothy party dress, to dance
till dawn in shiny patent shoes.

Waste not, want not. Mend and make do.

On winter nights you'd patiently unravel
the sleeves of jumpers, knit them back,
cut out the thin, frayed yarn. Often
you took two tattered sheets
and stitched one new.

Close to eighty now, you stick to old tricks
to auld claes and porritch.

So when death unravels you
I'll inherit cupboards full of virgin linen,
bales of pastel towels wrapped in dusty cellophane,
thirties suits and forties frocks and fifties shoes, like new.

I'll dress you then in a pale silk gown
six thousand silkworms died to spin.
I'll gently comb your hair. I'll set
your fine wool hat upon your head,
your finest string of pearls around your neck.
And on your grave I'll leave
armfuls of cut flowers.

Last Night Old Age Visited Me

Last night Old Age visited me,
stood boldly by my side, while I looked
in the mirror's cold glass eye.

I did not like to stare, but
neither could I tear my eyes away
from her reflection. She stood,
naked like me, and I saw her whole life
written on her skin –

the blemish by her navel
raspberry at birth, more radish now
the shining scar on her left shin
where she'd fallen as a child
and run home sobbing to her mother's knee

the jab mark from her BCG,
the freckles where the sun had kissed
when once she'd sunbathed naked as a leaf

the lines a growing child had drawn
in white across her abdomen,
the slug trails of a surgeon's blade,
the varicose worm her third child made

the milk-white breasts that once had filled with love
the patch of hair which once she'd shaved
to a shining, black, heart Valentine,
the belly skin his hands had stroked,
once firm and tight, now slackening.

I got a fright when she spoke.

Move over, she said, her voice strong as a girl's.
You're in my place. I'm going out tonight.
I've not got time to stand and stare. I need to fix my face.

And next thing I knew she was
brushing colour on her cheeks and lips,
slipping those milk-white breasts in silken cups,
sliding skimpy panties on her hips,
letting down her auburn hair.

Don't wait up, she called as she slammed the door,
I'm frisky as a pup tonight – I'm going to score.

On Beltane Night

On Beltane night
we'll take the car
up the Takmadoon

Right up in the hills
when we no longer see
the orange glow of Glasgow
or headlights trickling through
the Kelvin valley miles below
we'll stop by the side
of a cold black loch

On Beltane night
we'll hold each other close
rekindle the ancient flame

We'll count the stars
until the hungry dawn
guzzles them one by one

We'll think on what has been
of what is still to come

she drinks it down

she drinks it down
in gulping mouthfuls

exquisite as
salt oysters sliding slow
over lips, tongues, throat

cool as chilled white wine

the love of a good man
the ultimate
divine

Just Like Eve

I could have brought you
whisky to warm you on winter nights,
poems full of words to fill your silences

I could have brought you
armfuls of flowers
to fill your rooms with summer,
scented petals to scatter where you dream

I could have brought
olives, shiny, black and green,
anchovies and Parmesan,
Chianti, deep blood-red

I could have brought
figs, dates, kumquats, lychees
tastes to make your senses sing
to set your soul adrift

Instead I brought
forbidden fruit
the one and only gift
you would not accept

Because I Want You So Much (You Bastard)

I have a car and a credit card
and you're not that far away
another country but only
a few hundred miles between lovers and
I could easily phone in sick
put the key in the ignition, stick
in your favourite CD
fill up at the petrol station
with diet coke and a bag of chocolate raisins
and somewhere on the road –
the slip lane to the M8 –
I'll see this young hitchhiker
and I'll stop and pick him up
because if I'm on my way to you
then it's fate I'll get there safe
so I'll maniac-drive the fast lane
wipers swishing wildly
against the rainbow trail
of juggernauts at ninety
my heart on a helium high
because you're fucking wonderful.

But I think I'll phone before I go
and I smile at the joke on your machine –
that sexy, female voice, orgasmic-edged,
pussy-purring down the line.

But though I wait she never says
Please Leave Your Message After The Tone
instead she calls for you and says
some woman wants you on the phone.

But I've got a car and a credit card
and I need the coke and the raisins
and a fix from a six-inch chocolate bar
and maybe that hitchhiker's waiting
on the sliplane to my future
so I'll go and I'll stop and I'll pick him up
and say, mate, you're in luck
and maybe that's not safe
for a female on her own, but
since you're a bastard **and** I still want you
I couldn't give a fuck.

Fruit Machine

I wink at the fruit machine –
it winks back – orange, red, green
while I sit drinking long, cool
glasses of iced loneliness.

The guy in the corner thinks
I'm winking at him. Over he ambles
one hand clutching a half-drunk pint
the other jingling pennies in his pocket
as if he thinks I'm easy as a wean at a wedding
waiting for the scramble.

I do not return his hot, hungry glance.
I'm staring at the fruit machine,
the man has not a chance.

Coldness floods from me, tangible as the cold
from an open freezer door
and he's a fool in a short-sleeved shirt
trudging through the Tundra of my glower.

So what does he do?
Slides between me and my machine.
Stands legs akimbo, thrusts his groin
against its metal hips, slips a coin
between its metal lips
presses the right buttons

and suddenly it's
orgasmic
flashing and wailing
and screaming out for more

If only women were so simple, eh?

Love Is . . .

LUV is a cheap three letter word
when found in valentines.
L.O.V.E's a bitter acronym –
Lean Over Vertiginous Edges and
bet your satin-padded scented heart
someone will end up hurt.

Stirred and shaken in a *tin*
then whipped into a froth
love will end up *violent*
so, once consumed, dispose of
with great care, the sharpened edges
of a tin can cause a nasty tear.

Or what if LOVE's an anagram?
The vole is not a pet
you'd choose to let inside your home
let alone your heart.

But must love be so bleak
blood-red romantics sigh,
so don't despair, love can be found,
and I know where
for as I live and move around
LOVE's tattooed on my thigh!

Wicked Spell

Who can I blame? Was it some fairy
cast a wicked spell
caused me to lose my heart
and my common sense as well?

I was careless, so careless,
like a child with her mittens,
like a country girl with her purse.

Foolish princess playing by the well
I let my heart bounce off
like a jewelled golden ball
and gladly told the toad
I'd trade him anything
if he would let me have it back again.

Ugly toad.
How many times did I close my eyes
and kiss your warty cheek.
How many times did I let you share my bed
and lie and listen to your grunts and wake
at dawn and gaze at you –
AND YOU WERE STILL A TOAD!

Now I'm alone and lonely as the Lady of Shallot
locked in my bungalow
behind my double glazing and my festoon blinds
weaving pictures of the world
through the mirror of my eyes
the mirror of this page
too timid, not sufficiently brave
to turn and face reality . . .

Everything is breaking.
The mirror cracks.
I accuse myself
of bringing seven years bad luck.

Tupperware Torture

Five points for the lady who's wearing red shoes
three for she who can mend a fuse. . .

The demonstrator drones and bores us all –
or does she?
This is how she breaks the ice,
the game to put us at our ease,
laugh politely – we must please
the hostess. After all, she is a friend –
at least, she once was.

The plastic tubs are laid out on the floor,
we housewives have our chance to test and try.
Can no-one hear me as I dumbly cry?
Why did I come to this,
to being here
suburban wife and mindless bore?

The agent smiles and demonstrates her wares
the plastic lids she operates with ease
there's one for butter, one for cheese,
freeze your bananas, chips, eclairs –
is there anyone who really cares?
I gulp a yawn.
This is one.

I dream to free me from this deadening state
my heads afloat, my thoughts lazily drifting. . .
so what's this plastic lid that I see lifting?
It zooms in closer –
could be I'm mad –
I've seen a flying saucer.
It isn't easy to think straight
face to face with a plastic plate
but I've been asked to demonstrate
their latest lid
and though I try to concentrate
I think I've flipped mine.

So sorry, but my mind had wandered –
gone – in fact. A guilty child caught by surprise
I shrink away from neighbours' eyes,
fear what they are thinking.
Or are they?
I wish that I could rise and flee

anywhere to be set free
from some friends livingroom
awash in Tupperware –
I'm in deep and sinking.

Containers stagnate sterile on a shelf –
if this is life then let me kill myself!
I'll stick my head in their super breadbin
they guarantee no air gets in
for five years.
Or stick me in a big square round
and shove me six feet underground
I'll keep quite fresh
so shed no tears
be no more dead than I've been for years
but well-preserved
that's guaranteed
if not deserved.
I know the score
suburban life's a mindless chore.

Five points for the lady whose shoes are red
Three for she who has never wed
No points for the girl who's good in bed
and death to any with thoughts in her head

The ice has broken.
I have fled.

Confessions of a Wild Woman

Dear God
Who art in HQ somewhere in America
Let me confess the sins
Which have made me the miserable witch
I deserve to be

Everything is my fault
As it always was
And so will surely always be . . .

In my house are many rooms
And it is hard to hoover and clean them all

And in a secret cupboard I hoard a Himalaya
Of ironing, which has been known to avalanche
Causing danger to life and limb
And the temporary loss of one small child

But worse than these Oh Lord I must confess
I own a black and lacy thong
And a clingy backless dress

I have long hair and legs and cause men to lust after me
Especially if the light is low and their vision failing
And now, Oh Lord, even with the greying of the hair
And the lengthening of the tooth
And the lowering of bum and boobs
I get drunk on Saturdays
And fornicate on Sundays when I should be in church

I hide from The Christian Aid woman
When she calls for her envelope
And dodge the Big Issue Seller at the corner
But only if I don't have change

I use foul language
But only when sorely pressed
Or pissed

I harbour ill-thoughts towards my fellow men
Especially those at work

I covet the Diet Coke Man
And the young guy at the bus stop
Whose shy smile brightens my day
With heathen and unnatural thoughts

Sometimes I forget to water my houseplants
And they die
Sometimes I over-water my houseplants
And they die

And for these sins, Oh kind and loving God
Who is all-powerful, all-loving and all-forgiving
I deserve no better than to bring forth
In sweat and blood and agony and suffering
He who now borrows my car without asking.

I deserve no better than to be paid
A miserable salary for doing
A miserable job

While still trying to mother the fruits of my sins
And somewhere inbetween sing the praises of He
Who made me from mud and rib

So please forgive me,
Oh mother and father who brought me up right
And John Knox who lurketh like a flasher
in the shadows of my mind
For I have sinned
And am not finished yet.

Biographical Note

Magi Gibson was educated at Kilsyth Academy, then Glasgow University. She graduated from university with an MA in French and German at the age of nineteen and while still just twenty began teaching at Cumbenauld High School. She spent a year in Paris teaching English as a foreign language.

After the births of her first two children she started writing and became a creative writing tutor with the Workers Educational Association. She dabbled in politics, but after the birth of her third child and a serious illness, she decided against pursuing a career in politics. Her social and political concerns still shine through in her writing.

From 1992-1994 Magi was a Scottish Arts Council Writing Fellow with Renfrew District Council. She then returned to teaching for five years and specialised in working with children with social, emotional and behavioural difficulties. As a tutor with the WEA and with Artlink Central she has worked in both men's and women's prisons. She co-wrote a playscript with women in Cornton Vale Prison as part of an Artlink multimedia project. The play was performed in 1998 in the prison.

She is currently the SAC Writing Fellow for Aberdeenshire and is taking part in a project in Angus exploring the teaching of environmental education through expressive arts.

Magi Gibson's poetry has been widely published in Scottish literary magazines and anthologies as well as in magazines in England and Ireland and in anthologies with worldwide distribution. She was the co-winner of the *Scotland on Sunday/* Women 2000 writing prize in 1990.

She has previously published one full-length collection of poetry, *Kicking Back*, (Taranis), which was nominated for the Saltire Best First Book Award.

An accomplished performer of her work, Magi has travelled throughout Scotland for readings. When everything gets a bit too hectic, and before her children and husband forget what she looks like, she rushes back to her home near the Lake of Menteith on the edge of the Trossachs in South Perthshire.

She has never been to Macduff with Springsteen, but if he should by any chance read the poem for him in this collection, she is willing to do the driving and pay for the Irn Bru.